Contents

The world is full of light and colour 2

Many things give us light 4

You see light with your eyes 6

You need light to see things 8

Light shines through some things 10

Light makes shadows 12

Light makes reflections 14

Light can be different colours 16

You can see many colours 18

There are many shades of colour 20

Colour helps us 22

Index 24

2

The world is full of light and colour.

Many things give us light.

The sun gives us light in the daytime.
A candle can give us light.
A torch can help you to see in the dark.
A car has lights to use at night.
We switch lights on at night.

Focus

light
sun
candle
torch

NEVER look at the Sun. It will hurt your eyes.

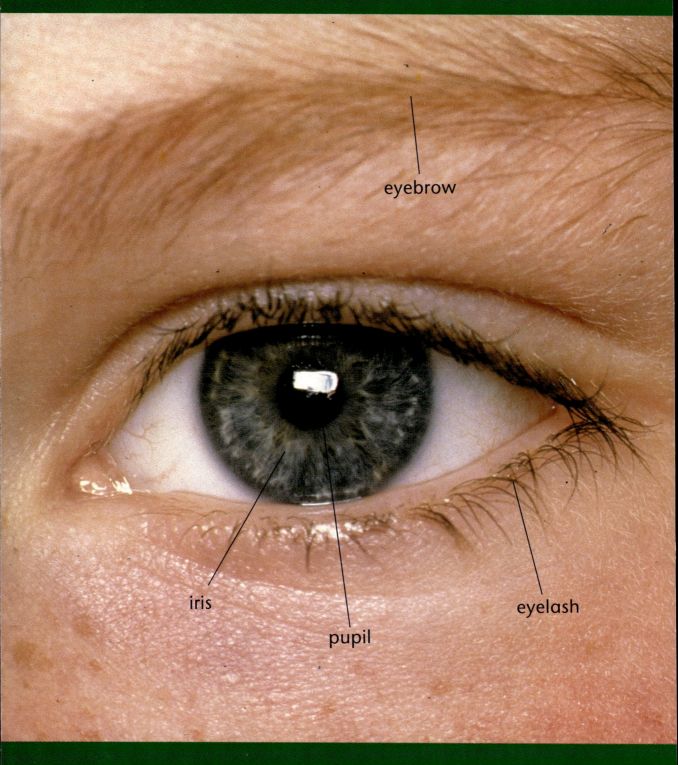

You see light with your eyes.

Light goes into your eyes through a small 'hole'.
The 'hole' is the black part of your eye.
The 'hole' is called the pupil.
Light goes in through the pupil so you can see.
Without light you cannot see.

Focus
pupil

A cat's pupils are not always round.

You need light to see things.

When it is dark it is hard to see.
When it is dark a torch helps you to see.
The torch shines light on the toy car.
Then you can see the car is red.

What other things can you see in the torchlight?

Focus
light
dark
torch
shine

You can see light, but you cannot feel, hear, smell, or taste it.

Light shines through some things.

Sunlight shines through a window.
A window is made from glass.
You can see through the glass.
Glass is a transparent material.

Do you know any other transparent materials?

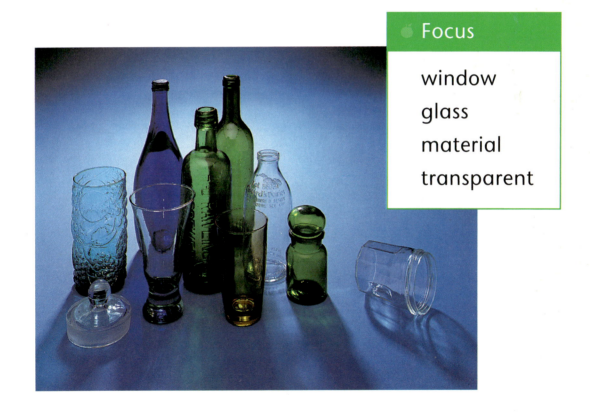

Focus

window
glass
material
transparent

Some things make shadows.

Some things do not let light through.
They make shadows.
You can make shadows on a sunny day.
You can make a shadow if you block out the sunlight.
You can use a torch to make shadows.

What shadows can you make?

 Focus

shadow
opaque

Materials you cannot see through are called opaque.

A shiny spoon can make a funny reflection.

Light makes reflections.

Light bouncing off something shiny makes a reflection.
A mirror is shiny.
When you look into a mirror the picture you see is you.
The picture is your reflection.

Look for reflections in other shiny things.

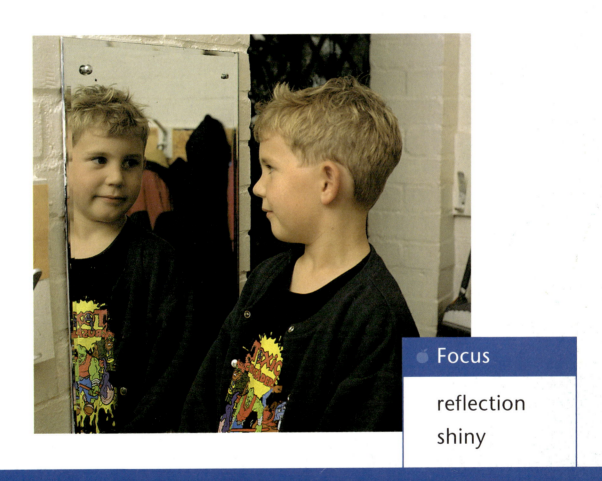

Focus

reflection
shiny

Light can be different colours.

A police car has a blue light.
A bicycle has a red light.
Traffic lights have three colours.

Can you think of some coloured lights?

Focus

traffic lights

When it rains and the sun shines it makes a rainbow with seven colours.

You can see many colours.

Some colours are bright.
Some colours are dull.

What colours can you see?

Do you have a favourite colour?

> Focus
>
> colours
> bright
> dull

19

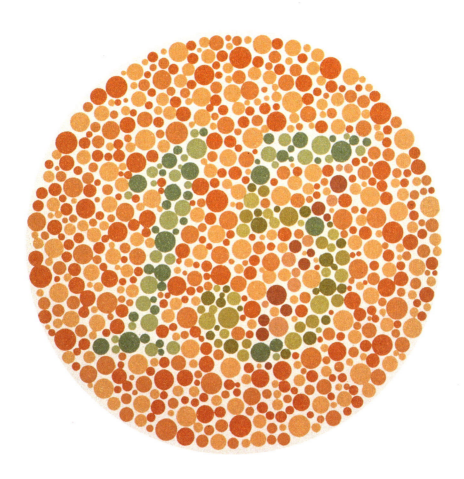

Some people cannot see all colours. They are colour blind. Do you see 15 or 17 in the big circle?

There are many shades of colour.

These things are all green.
Some are light green.
Some are dark green.
They are different shades of green.

Can you see shades of red?

Can you see shades of blue?

- **Focus**

  shade
  light
  dark

Some animals do not see colours.
Dogs see everything as black, white, and grey.

Using colour for hiding is called camouflage.

Colour helps us.

Colour can help us to be seen.
Colour can help us to hide.
Colour can warn us of danger.
Some animals use colour to be seen.
Some animals use colour to hide.

Can you see the moth?

● Focus

hide
camouflage

Index

camouflage 22
colour 3, 17, 18, 19, 21, 23, 24
colour blind 19

dark 5, 9
daytime 5

eyes 7

light 3, 5, 7, 9, 11, 13, 15, 17

mirror 15

night 5

opaque 13

pupil 6, 7

rainbow 17
reflection 15

shades of colour 21
shadow 13
shiny 15
sun 5
sunlight 11, 13

transparent 11

Oxford University Press, Walton Street, Oxford OX2 6DP

Oxford New York Toronto Delhi
Bombay Calcutta Madras Karachi
Kuala Lumpur Singapore Hong Kong
Tokyo Nairobi Dar es Salaam Cape Town Melbourne Auckland Madrid
and associated companies in Berlin Ibadan

Oxford is a trademark of Oxford University Press

© Linda Dixon 1993

First printed in 1993

Printed in France
by Pollina, 85400 Luçon - n° 63457M

ISBN Paperback 019 918311 2

A CIP catalogue record for this book is available from the British Library.

All rights reserved. No part of this publication may be reproduced, stored in a retrieval system, or transmitted, in any form or by any means, without prior permission in writing of Oxford University Press. Within the UK, exceptions are allowed in respect of any fair dealing for the purpose of research or private study, or criticism or review, as permitted under the Copyright, Designs and Patents Act, 1988, or in the case of reprographic reproduction in accordance with the terms and licences issued by the Copyright Licensing Agency. Enquiries concerning reproduction outside those terms and in other countries should be sent to the Rights Department, Oxford University Press, at the address above.

Acknowledgements

The publisher wishes to thank the following for permission to reproduce photographs:

Animal Photography /Sally Anne Thompson p 21; Bruce Coleman Ltd /Jane Burton p 7 (left); Cull photographic pp 10, 12, 15, 23; Chris Honeywell pp 5, 11, 14, 20; NHPA /G I Bernard p 22; Science Photo Library pp 6, /Adam Hart-Davis 19; Tony Stone Photolibrary-London front cover, /David Olsen p 17; Zefa pp 4, 7 (right).
Page 19 reproduced from Ishihara's Tests for Colour Blindness published by Kanehara & Co Ltd., Tokyo, Japan.

The illustrations are by David Barnett.

Coordinating author: **Terry Jennings**
Language consultant: **Diana Bentley**
Additional contributions: **Nick Axten**
Claire Axten